CW00567484

POCKETS FULL
OF STRING

First Published in Great Britain 2021 by Mirador Publishing

Copyright © 2021 by Jan Millward

All rights reserved. No part of this publication may be reproduced or transmitted, in any form or by any means, without permission of the publishers or author. Excepting brief quotes used in reviews.

First edition: 2021

Any reference to real names and places are purely fictional and are constructs of the author. Any offence the references produce is unintentional and in no way reflects the reality of any locations or people involved.

A copy of this work is available through the British Library.

ISBN: 978-1-913833-72-5

Mirador Publishing
10 Greenbrook Terrace
Taunton
Somerset
TA1 1UT

POCKETS FULL OF STRING

BY

JAN MILLWARD

INTRODUCTION

Living through a pandemic has had some odd perks. It has given me the time, if not the energy to finally put together another little book of rural rhymes. Many of the poems in this book have been shared on social media and I have had some lovely comments on how they have brought a little joy in what has been a very traumatic time for so many of us.

I am sure some of you will relate to the tales told here and I do hope you enjoy reading them. If I can make you smile, my job is done!

Jan Millward

Stand in the Gap

It's funny how useful you become when there are animals on the loose! I am used to being put in a gap in the hedge and told to wait for my moment to shine!

All those years at college,
All the time in school,
Hours in the classroom
I don't think that I'm a fool.

I'm not too bad at writing,
I don't get in a flap.
But sometimes what I'm best at
Is standing in a gap.

Whenever there is trouble
Or the gates been left ajar,
And the heifers are escaping
And they've gone pretty far.

I get an urgent phone call:
"The bulls have had a scrap.
They've broken down the fence,
Can you please stand in the gap?

Forget the cake you're making
Just grab your boots and coat,
I'll get you on the quad bike
But don't hang on to my throat".

It can happen in the evening
Or at the break of day
Or at the stroke of midnight
Or whilst they're making hay.

I must be rather useful
At waving a big stick.
And filling gaps in hedgerows
Or the lane behind the rick.

The sheep all like escaping
Just as I'm making tea,
And I never get a second
To even have a wee.

But my response is rapid
I am like a well coiled spring,
I have wellies at the ready
And pockets full of string.

Forget those nice diplomas
They really aren't much use
When all you hear is "Help us,
The cattle have got loose"!

THE OLD TRACTOR

There is something very poignant about ancient abandoned tractors rusting quietly away in hedgerows.

I am a poor old tractor
Abandoned near a wood,
But I was once a work horse
I'd tell you if I could.

I ploughed the fields and scattered
The good seed on the land,
Oiled and greased and ready
To help my old farm hand.

We harrowed the old meadow,
We rolled the gentle glen.
We chugged along the byways,
The world was different then.

Churns were in the trailer,
Straw was in a stook.
Gentle honest farming,
Not learnt from any book.

But the wind was changing
And I had been replaced,
With modern new machinery
And I was left to waste.

Abandoned near the gateway
The rust soon took its toll,
My tyres went flat and useless
My engine leaked out oil.

The brambles tried to hide me
As if they were ashamed,
And soon I was forgotten
Old ways forever changed.

They bought a brand-new combine
And had to move the gate,
Once more I was discovered,
A long-forgotten mate.

No paintwork on my panels,
No wheel to steer me by.
No way to start my engine,
No one would even try.

Now I am just a memory,
I'll never pull the plough.
I look out in amazement
At those that pull them now.

But once I was amazing,
Once I was brand new.
Once I was the engine
That others came to view.

Remember time keeps turning,
It never is too late
To grasp the joy of living
Before you're parked up by the gate.

GENTLY FROM THE PLOUGH

It may be many years since horses were used to plough the land and even more years have passed since they were used in war. Let's spare a moment to remember those gentle giants.

Gently went the farmer's plough horse
Off to feed the fields of war.
No one knew where they were going
No one knew what lay in store.

Muzzle soft and gently breathing,
Faithful to the bitter end.
Just another into battle,
a loyal, trusting soldier's friend.

Pulling guns towards the front line,
Scared and sore through wire and mud.
Honest heart and trusting nature,
Witness to the guns and blood.

Soldiers tried to use compassion
But they knew the price of pain.
Onwards fighting for our freedom,
Was it really all in vain?

All those horses, all the carnage
Worn, discarded as they fell
abandoned then, but we'll remember
Their long journey through that hell.

All the lives and all the fallen
Long ago on foreign soil,
Helped us to hang on to freedom
Never doubting, heavy toil.

Victory earnt so very bravely
The cost was high; the fight was long.
Remember if you will the horses
The innocents that knew no wrong.

MARY

Mary is quite different to the six pampered hens at the bottom of my garden!

Mary was a battery hen
She laid her eggs each day at ten.
Ten thousand others in her shed
Always warm and always fed.

She didn't know that there was more
Not far away outside the door.
She ate her food and had a drink,
Because she wasn't bred to think.

At night, the lights were dimmed quite low,
She never heard a cockerel crow.
No perch for her, no day or night
No room to stretch as if in flight.

Then someone said this isn't fair,
We need to think a bit and care.
The chickens need to have the space
to spread their wings, it's a disgrace.

And when some farmers saw the harm,
They tried to free range poultry farm
Where hens could scratch and get outside
And if it rained could run and hide.

Yes, it costs more for happy hens
It takes more space for bigger pens,
But surely it is worth the price.
and free-range eggs, they taste so nice.

So, Mary's life was not in vain,
Now many hens feel sun and rain.
They scratch around for worms and seeds,
Not feeding others greedy needs.

We all must think and have the choice,
Vote with our feet and have a voice.
Take the time to check the labels
And buy the best that you are able.

THE HEREFORD LOOK

I would definitely be a Hereford if somehow I ended up reincarnated as a cow!

I've never rocked that perfect look,
No part of me is from a book
And if I try and give a pout
My husband thinks that I've got gout.

My hair is thick and going grey,
My chubby belly's here to stay.
My bingo wings could almost fly
It isn't fair, I always try.

I've cut down on the bread and toast
And all the foods I love the most.
I walk and trot and nearly run,
(whoever said that could be fun).

But there's a devil in my head
Who tempts me to eat chips instead.
It seems I'm destined to be dumpy,
There's not much point in being grumpy.

It seems that breeding plays its part
Our fate is destined from the start.
Some things in life we cannot change,
A skinny me would be so strange.

If I came back as a sweet cow
I don't know when, I don't know how.
Hereford would be my breed,
Always looking for a feed.

The jersey cows with doleful eyes
Are never sent off to make pies.
They are so sleek, so lean, and pretty
All I can try to be is witty!

HE'S GONE

I was asked to write a poem for a farmer's funeral and this is it.

He's in the breeze and winters rain.
He's left the land, his soul remains.
It looks the same, each hill and tree,
He was so very dear to me.
His boots still lie by the back door
His gentle voice we'll hear no more.
No "put the kettle on for tea"
His pain is gone; he's been set free
His precious farm was all his life
With Betty here, his own dear wife.
We didn't want to say goodbye,
It's hard to stand here and not cry.
He loved his sheep; he knew them all
The cattle, they came to his call.
The crops he grew to feed his stock,
He was our Dad, our hope, our rock.
A proper countryman at heart
He knew he'd farm right from the start.
Dedication was the key,
This farm will be his legacy.
And we will promise to be true,
He knew what we would have to do.

We'll carry on and do our best,
Now is the time for him to rest.
Dear God, we hand you now our Dad,
We're trying hard to not be sad.
Protect and guide us through the years
And help us wipe away the tears.
And every now and then we'll smile,
It may take us a little while.
We will remember him each day
And think about the things he'd say.

THANKS TO THE FARMERS

A small thank you to all of you who work the land.

Thanks to all of you in wellies,
Growing food to fill our bellies.
Thanks for all the long hard days
Getting in those fields of maize.

Thanks for all those days of muck,
the times you're feeling out of luck.
the days your wellies always leak,
the keeping going week on week.

The times you had to call the vet,
the running up of yet more debt.
the cows you've milked, the calves you've fed
when all you wanted was your bed.

Thank you for the harvest home,
Contractors speed dial on the phone.
All those days of working late
helps put the food upon our plate.

And when you're stuck behind a baler,
a tractor and a heavy trailer
please be patient in the queue
just take your time, enjoy the view.

TO THE TUNE "MY OLD MAN'S A DUSTMAN"

(Yes, I do sing to my chickens, even more so when we are in lock down)!

I'm singing to my chickens,
They're still roaming free
If I keep singing to them
I'll get an egg for tea.
I'm singing to my chickens
I think I've got the knack
Cause every time I'm out there
They keep on singing back!

So, if you're feeling lonely
Sing to this simple song,
My chickens they will hear you
And they will sing along.
Dance around the kitchen
Skip around the hall,
Sing up for my chickens
And you will have a ball.

I'm singing to my chickens
They're still roaming free
If I keep singing to them
I'll get an egg for tea.

I'm singing to my chickens,
I think I've got the knack
Cause every time I'm out there
They keep on singing back!

The sun it is still shining
There's blossom on the trees,
Look out for the birdies
The butterflies and bees.
Clean out all your cupboards
Paint that grubby wall
Ring your friends and neighbours
And give someone a call

I'm singing to my chickens
They're still roaming free,
If I keep singing to them
I'll get an egg for tea.
I'm singing to my chickens
I think I've got the knack
Cause every time I'm out there
They keep on singing back!

AFTER CHRISTMAS
Guilty as charged!

After Christmas, every year
I say I'll get my ass in gear,
And run and cycle every day
then watch the pounds melt away.

The fridge is stocked with carrot sticks
I know the rules, learned all the tricks.
No carbs for me, I'm in the zone
Fighting the flab, stone by stone.

I hoover up the after eight,
Pringles and cheese meet the same fate.
Temptation must be kept at bay,
Just one more box left of Milk Tray.

Day one I'm ready, here we go
I would go out, but we've got snow.
By half past eight I've hunger pains
But as they say no pain, no gain.

By lunch, my stomach's asking please
for crusty bread and lumps of cheese.
But I am strong and tell it no,
Thin watery soup's the way to go.

My husband's eating cheese on toast
And asking if we're having a roast.
I suck a frozen grape and try
To not break down and scream or cry.

After a week, I'm on the scales
Another of my lifelong fails.
I've been so good, but I've put on,
I thought at least a pound had gone.

I'd told myself it's now or never
But now I'm waiting for the weather.
No one need run through fields of mud
Or push a bike through a deep flood.

But last night all the cows got out,
You should have heard them baul and shout
Five hours we ran 'cross hill and vale
Wrapped up against the sleet and hail.

The next day I am feeling smug,
Sipping my lemon in a mug.
I'm stiff and tired, and feeling ratty
But I 'm just a tiny bit less fatty.

So onwards I will face the battle
And exercise out with the cattle,
And try and put less in my gob
And not be such a lazy slob.

To all you ladies in this boat
Slow and steady gets my vote.
The fight is real, just do your best
And don't go shopping when you're stressed.

THE SUMMER BANK HOLIDAY

The summer bank holiday is peak harvest period and whilst the roads are usually packed with holiday makers, there is plenty of work to do on the farm.

The motorway is looking busy,
Mums are getting in a tizzy.
Picnics packed, buckets and spades
Umbrellas for the shade.

Cars loaded up with bats and balls
And first aid kits for scrapes and falls.
Sun cream to protect fair skin
Cans of beer, bottles of gin.

Towels laid out upon the sand,
Everyone is looking tanned.
A paddle in amongst the waves,
Costumes for those feeling brave.

Ice cream drips down sticky hands
In seaside towns across the land.
Rubber rings and sticks of rock,
Little boats trying to dock.

Nets for fishing out small crabs,
Sarongs to cover up the flab.
Seagulls searching for some chips,
A chance to go off on a trip.

A windbreak to mark out a patch,
Frisbees for a game of catch.
Deckchairs hired out for the day,
As yachts sail out across the bay.

A pleasant breeze begins to blow,
Heads and shoulders start to glow.
Sand in shoes and stuck in hair,
no one seems to have a care.

The day is done, the sun hangs low
it's nearly time to pack and go.
Tired and weary little heads,
dreaming of their comfy beds.

The roads fill up with miles of cars
whilst couples drink in pubs and bars.
Memories stored for winter days
of summer's special golden haze.

And whilst the queues wind up the road
The farmers gather in their loads.
Tired and dusty, out again
Filling the barns with golden grain.

BE THE ONE

Be strong when life can seem unfair,
Be kind and always show you care.
Be brave and stand up for your rights,
Be strong and always seek the light.

Be gentle, always choose your words,
Be sure the weakest voice is heard.
Be fearless in the darkest night,
Be funny, laugh with all your might.

Be daft and weird and love a lot.
Be thankful for the stuff you've got.
Be joyful for the good you see,
Be sure to live a life that's free.

Be smart when others block your way,
Be tough and always have your say.
Be tolerant to those who doubt,
Be sure to find the right way out.

Be a friend to those in need,
Regardless of beliefs and creed.
Be the one who stands up tall,
Be sure to get up when you fall.

Be the change in your small way,
Be the hope that's here to stay.
Be the one who dares to dream,
Be the stitch that mends the seam.

THE TRACTOR DRIVER

Kind and funny trumps waxed and polished every time in my book!

He isn't like men on the screen
With perfect looks and nails so clean.
He doesn't drive a flashy car,
He'll never be a movie star.

He doesn't have the perfect hair,
It looks a mess, he doesn't care.
He isn't an acknowledged actor
But he knows how to drive a tractor.

His tan ends halfway up his arms
From living life out on the farm.
He doesn't buy bouquets of flowers,
He works the land for hours and hours.

His hands are rough, his jeans are worn,
He wears a coat; the sleeves are torn.
He doesn't pluck or preen or wax,
He's pretty useful with an axe.

He often comes in from the fields
And talks about the latest yields.
He's just a good old-fashioned guy
who's partial to my apple pie.

But he is faithful, he is true
He makes me laugh when I am blue.
He's in my heart, he's in my soul,
He's picked me up and made me whole.

And when you see men on the screen
All buffed and polished, neat, and clean.
Remember love's worth more than money
Go for a man who's kind and funny!

THE ROGUE SOCK

I am sure everyone can relate to this!

There is little more annoying
And this always make me frown,
When I find out that I'm wearing
A sock that's falling down.

Some days it never happens
Some days slip by just fine,
But this day was a bad one,
and I need a glass of wine.

The fields were very muddy
so, I leaned against a gate.
Shaking off my dirty welly,
well, that was tempting fate.

One foot was really cosy,
That sock was still in place.
I tried to pull the other
but fell flat on my face.

I cursed the ground I sat on,
I even blamed the dog
soon I was standing barefoot
In something like a bog.

The sock went in my pocket
And my foot was cold and damp,
Mud oozed right through my welly
And I developed cramp.

Now I was really cranky
Frostbite was setting in
The sock pushed in my pocket
was destined for the bin.

I'd started off so happy
A little ray of light,
now I was cold and filthy
And looking quite a fright.

No one had best approach me,
and please nobody laugh.
Wait 'till I'm home and soaking
in a long-awaited bath.

REMEMBER

Talking about the weather is part of the job description when you work on the land!

Remember all the moaning when it was hot and dry?
When all the birds were singing, not a cloud up in the sky?
Remember how we suffered with sweaty boobs and brows,
And the farmers had a meltdown with no grass left for their cows?

Remember how we wilted under the baking summer's sun,
And the seaside towns were bursting with children having fun?
The ground was dry and cracking, the rivers had stopped flowing,
The crops were looking stunted and many had stopped growing.

And just a few weeks later we are stuck in a deep flood.
We can't get through the gateways; the dust has turned to mud.
The winds are blowing wildly, and the leaves have blocked the drains
And every time we go out it just rains and rains and rains.

And soon will come the warnings and the north winds start to blow
And everyone will panic because they think that it might snow.
You can't buy your normal shopping; the shelves are all stripped bare.
No milk, no cheese no carrots, it's enough to make you swear.

Then they tell you on the tele' that the snow will be so deep
That you'll need to take a shovel so that you can find your sheep.
We watch for the stinging blizzard and wrap up against the storm
And make sure all our livestock are safe and fed and warm.

The sheds are full of firewood, the fire is burning bright
We're ready for this weather on the long cold winter's night.
then we wake up one bright morning and see a sign of spring,
Just a tiny shoot uncurling bringing life to everything.

Life goes round in a circle, and the swallows will come back
And the mud dries in the gateways, there'll be daisies on the track.
We will look out for the promise that the spring is on its way
And we'll grease up the old baler for when we cut the hay.

So, batten down the hatches because this time will also pass,
And the cows will be back grazing on fields of lush green grass.
Because life is like the weather, we must ride out all the storms,
and store the sunny memories in our hearts to keep us warm.

THE APPLE

Sometimes it's the little memories that are the most poignant.

He never said I love you,
No airy fairy words
But he showed me nature's beauty
The trees, the hills, the birds.

I followed in his footsteps,
I watched him work the land.
I learned from every challenge
And now I understand.

He taught me life's main lessons,
That the animals come first.
However tired and hungry,
However, wracked with thirst

And I knew every gatepost,
And how to shut it tight,
How to walk a field so softly
And just know when all was right.

I learned the art of listening,
how to spot a sickly cow.
I still see him watching quietly,
I wish he was here right now.

He kept a pen knife in his pocket
And he'd pick some food for free.
Take a slice off a sweet apple
And pass it on to me.

And now the days are passing
The leaves are falling fast,
And the memory of that apple
Is one I know will last.

My Dad is still around me
He is in the wind and rain,
He'll be in the summer sunshine
Until we meet again.

I will always miss him,
But when I see that apple tree.
I'll smile and I'll remember
Just what he meant to me.

BLUE

The loss of your dog is a heartbreak many of us will relate to.

No hopeful whine,
no playful wag.
No holes chewed in
the shopping bag.

No muddy paws
across the hall,
no sleeping friend
curled in a ball.

No one to bark
when it is dark.
No more long walks
around the park.

No hopeful eyes
beside my chair,
no one to give
out love to share.

No hairs on carpets
and on jackets.
No one to shout at
"Shut that racket"

No one to lie
right on your feet,
no cold wet nose,
no scraps of meat.

no bounds of joy,
no rasping tongue.
Now he is gone
it feels so wrong.

The lead still hangs
up in the hall,
no one to catch
that small red ball.

No one to chase
the cats away,
no one to want
to always play.

THE CHANCE

This is what lock down does to a person, you start philosophising about your life choices, the universe, and acorns!

The oak tree hung heavy with acorns, secure in their perfect cups. Each one packed with potential, each one programmed for life.

The breeze passed carelessly through the branches, stirring the heavy crop.

A solitary acorn landed heavily on the track. Moments later it was crushed by a horse's hard hoof. Three more rattled on to the verge, one hit a rock on landing splitting its shell. The others lay exposed on the stony ground. They stayed where they fell and would soon shrivel and die.

A squirrel ran haphazardly up the trunk, gathering the ripe fruits ready to bury for his winter supplies. Another acorn landed nearby. It had a chance of growing there, but it would never reach its full potential as it would be hacked back each year to form part of the hedge. It would have a place but would never flourish like the mother tree.

The acorns landing on the field side had more protection. They had rich soil and the perfect start. Some would be eaten and picked off by the squirrels, others grazed off by wild deer in the spring.

Far away across the far side of the field in a small copse, a squirrel dug frantically into the leaf mould and left an acorn buried deep in the ground. It lay there undisturbed and unaffected by the world above.

The following spring, the squirrels were busy searching for their buried treasures. One by one, they dug up their acorns and filled their hungry bellies. The acorn in the copse however had been forgotten. Something incredible was about to happen. The conditions were perfect. It had everything it needed. Warmth, rich soil, water, and protection from the harsh world above.

The hard shell softened and cracked, and a tiny shoot grew towards the light. A few weeks later, two green leaves emerged, radiating delicately outwards towards the sun. None of the other acorns had had the chance to flourish. Many still lay rotting on the hard, unforgiving ground. But this one survived against all the odds.

For two hundred years it unfolded new leaves, steadily growing into a magnificent tree.

A small boy sat under the tree grateful for the shade from the late autumn sun. He picked up an acorn, examined it carefully and pushed it in his pocket. He planted it on his way home, burying it into the soft ground on the edge of the plain. The acorn was forgotten, but the power of the mighty oak was once again released.

Another two hundred years passed, and the boy was not even a memory, but the little acorn had flourished, and it now towered as a glorious tree on the edge of a busy housing estate.

Once again branches were heavy with acorns. The potential to survive in such a busy new world was limited, but still the acorns grew and once again a curious child picked up the seeds of a forest and playfully threw them into a wood on the edge of the play park.

THE IMAGE OF A FARMER

This was written after some ladies on Facebook spoke out about how there were still people who didn't believe that women worked on farms!

The image of a farmer
Is a man both strong and tough,
Who can wrestle with the cattle
And his skin is red and rough.

We see them on the tele'
In their checked and padded shirts.
Sleeves rolled up to elbows,
Boots covered in dirt.

It's not a job for women,
So many think that's true.
Driving great big tractors
Is not what the ladies do.

But you are much mistaken
As up and down the land,
The ladies are out farming
And they are doing grand.

So many single handed
Out there with their sheep,
Sorting out the cattle
Planting fields of wheat.

And some have little children
And they're coping all alone
Sorting out rotations
Ordering on the phone.

These mighty farming women
Know how to multitask
And if you want advice, well
You only have to ask.

Let's speak up for the women
Up and down the land,
Who are out there farming
They don't just lend a hand.

Farming is a life choice
And they need to get respect,
If you want to set a challenge
Well, you ain't seen nothing yet!

THE RAIN HAS STOPPED
Timing is everything!

The rain has stopped, the forecasts dry
The farmers check the bright blue sky.
It's getting late, but they must plough
The time is here, the time is now.

They need to cultivate and drill.
The wind has dropped, the trees are still
Before the winter storms set in
They plant the seed, they have to win.

For soon the skies will turn to grey
And they won't have another day.
Then they will work long through the night,
The fields will be ablaze with light.

Day by day and hour on hour
They plant the wheat to make our flour
With sandwiches and flasks of tea
Balanced on a dusty knee.

Tired and weary they go on
They watch the setting of the sun,
they keep on going will we sleep
What they plant they know they'll reap.

This is for those who work the land
Working on clay or loam or sand
Once it is drilled for daily bread
they can go down the pub instead!

WE ALL STILL NEED TO EAT

With grateful thanks to all of our keyworkers.

When the whole world nearly shut down
And the people stayed inside,
And we watched the television
To see how many died

We clapped for all the nurses
as we tried to work from home,
And we couldn't hug our loved ones
Or the ones left on their own.

We praised the supermarkets
For filling up the shelves,
and thanked the lorry drivers
for not thinking of themselves.

But out there in the country
the farmers didn't stop,
the fields still needed ploughing
they were planting a new crop.

The cows still needed milking
The sheep had to be fed.
Cattle wanted bedding
With straw inside their shed.

And whilst we all were watching
As the virus shut us down,
The farmers kept providing
Food for every town.

Because whatever we are facing
In every house and every street,
there's one thing that's for certain
we will always need to eat.

Wild Weeing
Most of us have been caught short at some time!

It's not so very easy if you need to use the loo
If you're out on a tractor, you know what you must do
You'll choose the nearest hedgerow or a big and handy tree
Where you can stoop in comfort and release a warm wild wee.

But if you're out there working with others on the farm,
You'll probably have to tell them, there really is no harm.
The men have got it easy, they just have to turn their backs
Whilst you are hunting cover along a rugged track.

The worst is open moorland or on a treeless fen,
That's when you know you'll want to wee and wee again.
Or if you've found a spot where you think you can't be seen
But you are in a hurry and you miss and hit your jeans

The worst is when you're desperate and really need to go
Then just around the corner walking oh so slow,
Is a couple with binoculars and a flask full of hot tea
Who stop and gaze around them to see what they can see.

Have you been caught by ramblers just as you start to stoop?
You might not hear them coming even though they're in a group
You could smile and wave and thank them and pretend you've
seen a bird
Even though you know you're gabbling and sounding quite absurd.

You must be very careful of nettles or a bramble.
Wee'ing in a gateway is also quite a gamble.
And if you need some paper, it's best to use a dock
And try to be discreet and not give the sheep a shock.

If you live in the country, you'll have wee'd in many fields
That little bit of nitrogen will have enhanced the yields
It's really not a problem, you'll have done it since a child
And know all those special places where to wee out in the wild!

CHASING SHEEP

The unwritten rule is that if the gate is open you leave it open. If it is shut, you make sure that it stays that way!

A merry blooming Christmas,
It's enough to make you weep,
When early Christmas morning
You are out there chasing sheep.

Someone had been out walking
And hadn't shut the gate,
We did the rounds quite early,
But we were still too late.

Miss Smith from down the village
Gave us an early call,
She'd taken out the rubbish
And found one in her hall.

She tried to control her panic
And shooed it with a brush,
But the ewe was going nowhere
it wasn't in a rush.

It nibbled on the ivy
That was coiled around the stairs,
then it peed a smelly puddle
and pushed under a chair.

The rest were in the church yard
Eating wreathes from off the graves,
The vicar was in melt down
He had many souls to save.

He said the Lord's my shepherd
but he still needs help from us,
and that day our dear old vicar
really found out how to cuss.

We had turned up in our PJ's
Wellies and a hat,
A coat dragged from the hallway
That was underneath the cat.

Miss Smith was in a panic
And had now called 999,
And the vicar started praying
For help that was divine.

The dog was very happy
To get an extra run,
But rounding up on Christmas
Isn't my idea of fun.

We got them in the paddock
And tied the gate with string,
Just as the bells for Christmas
Were getting set to ring.

Miss Smith was with the vicar
She was in a nervous state,
But next time she goes out early
Maybe she will shut the gate.

WOODLAND FAIRIES

Every now and then I enjoy writing a poem for children. I grew up in fairyland and sometimes I think I'm still there!

If you learn to love the woodlands
The flowers and the trees,
And listen to the bird song
You might see one of these.

Hiding in the bracken,
can you see how they uncurl?
You may get a glimpse of magic,
a moss green fairy girl.

Use your imagination
When the blue bells are in bloom,
Could they be bells or lanterns
To light a fairy room?

You may catch a tiny movement
From the corner of your eye.
A flash of woodland magic?
Or a sparkling dragonfly?

Look around the tree trunks
For moss spongy, dank, and green.
It is bedding for the wee folk,
A fine duvet for a queen.

If you tread very gently
And use your ears and eyes,
You will find all kinds of treasures
From the roots up to the skies.

The hazel's dusty catkins
Shakes pollen on the bees,
Maybe a woodland fairy
Has ridden one of these?

And if you find an oak tree
You may find some tiny cups,
Which the fairies use for parties
Far away from the grown-ups.

The little stars of stitchwort
So delicate and white,
May lead to a fairy kingdom
Where everything is bright.

And the webs spun by the spiders
Are made from tiny threads,
That the fairies use to stitch up
Daisy blankets for their beds.

If you peep around a tree stump
You may find a hazel shell.
If you put them in a puddle
They make a fairy boat as well.

And if you find a toadstool
It may be a tiny house.
Don't touch it or you'll spoil it,
Creep on past like a mouse.

And sometimes you may hear them
You may think that it's a bird,
But it might be fairy laughter,
Listen out for magic words.

They will fly up to a dandelion
And scatter them around.
Then float in on a seed head
and land gently on the ground.

The woods hold many secrets,
Listen to the trees.
You might just hear them whispering,
When there's a gentle breeze.

Remember you are walking
In a very special place,
The fairies know you love them
If you leave without a trace.

If you believe in magic
Go and see what you can find,
Respect the living creatures
And remember to be kind.

NEARLY CHRISTMAS

One for the pig farmers!

It may be nearly Christmas
But we can't all stay in bed,
If you have sheds of piggies
They'll be waiting to be fed.

Get out there in your wellies
In wind and rain or snow,
Hats pulled over eyebrows
Chilblains on each toe.

Pushing through the piglets
As they race around the shed,
Fluffing up their straw bales
Whilst the rest of us are in bed.

But it is so rewarding
To see pigs' content and warm,
Snuffling through their bedding
Protected from the storm.

MARRYING A FARMER

I was asked to write a poem about what it is like to marry into the farming life
to prepare a novice for what may lie in store!

Marrying a farmer is more than just the man
It's signing up for getting the famous farmer's tan.
It's cancelling your days out because it's turned out sunny,
It's realising that farmers have much more muck than money.

It's trips to pick up wormer and extra bags of feed,
String for the old baler and other stuff they need.
Its welly boots all covered in various types of muck,
I don't know why some people say it brings good luck.

There's always coming second to a lamb that needs a feed,
And getting the old tractor that isn't built for speed.
Milking cows and calving, sheeting up the pit
Straw stuck in your bra and the sweet smell of cow shit.

But if you really love him you both will understand
That farming is a lifetime of living on the land.
Don't care about the housework, don't stress about the mess
Today it may be overalls, tomorrow a posh dress.

Contented grunts and rustles,
you cannot help but smile
as you watch them rooting under
the straw raked in a pile.

Back in the house for breakfast
And if you have a bit of luck,
You won't walk through the kitchen
In boots covered in muck.

So have a happy Christmas,
But make sure you shut the gate
Or you might find your celebrations
Will be running a bit late!

I CANNOT DRAW

You don't have to be particularly good at something to enjoy doing it. This book is testimony to that!

I cannot draw, I cannot paint,
the thought of sewing makes me faint.
I cannot crochet, felt, or knit
I know my limits, I will quit.

I cannot ice those perfect cakes,
I really don't have what it takes.
I try, but only make a mess
and turn all blotchy with the stress.

I cannot do so many things,
Like making wreaths from wiry rings.
I cannot make things out of tweed
Or thread a string of pretty beads.

But I embroider in my mind,
And when I write it down, I find
I can paint pictures using words
I know it sounds a bit absurd.

Words can bring comfort, words can heal
I write down what I really feel.
I weave them into gentle rhymes
Some downright silly, others sublime.

Please never think what you can't do
Just look out at another view,
and you'll just know if it feels right
then you'll be happy day and night!

Remember you will say things when you are moving sheep,
the curses and the shouting might make a grown man weep.
But that is very normal don't take it all to heart
Sheep always are escaping; they really aren't that smart.

But farming has a habit of getting in your blood
It isn't always pretty, there's always lots of mud
So, off you go together, your new life has just begun
Full of joy and passion and a shovel full of fun!

THE OPEN GATE

Never underestimate Gran!

The parlour was ready for milking,
The yard was all scraped out and clean.
The tank was connected and cooling
But not a cow could be seen.

The gate to the back track was open
The cow at the front pushed on through,
The others followed behind her,
That's something that all cows will do.

She let out a very loud bellow
and kicked up a hell of a row,
Even the old ones were trotting
Each stroppy young heifer and cow.

Udders were swinging so wildly
Like pendulums under a clock,
But standing in the next gateway
Was granny in boots and a frock.

She'd been having a nap in the garden
But had spotted the breakaway herd,
She was stood on the path with a broomstick
Not a nerve was shaken or stirred.

The cowman was having a panic
his language hung blue in the air,
he could see his Gran in the distance
it was she who had taught him to swear.

Two hundred cows were advancing
Snorting and bellowing loud,
Heading straight for Gran's garden
But she would never be bowed.

She stood in front of the lead cow
and held up her broom to the sky.
she stood there for a few seconds
and stared them straight in the eye.

The brakes went on and they slowed down
And she turned around the whole herd,
One feisty little old granny
But she only uttered one word.

"Hup" she said, and they turned round,
She stood well clear of their tails.
Five foot two, what a woman
She'd knocked the wind from their sails.

They slowly went back to the parlour
And she wrapped some twine round the gate.
The cowman started the milking,
He was only a few minutes late.

The moral to this short story
is don't underestimate gran,
and any woman in farming
is at least a match for a man!

TURN OUT
Another one written during lockdown!

If you've ever worked with cattle
You will know what fun that brings,
But the best part is the turn out
When winter turns to spring.

All through the cold wet weather
They are kept out of the mud,
Protected from the elements
When we have had a flood.

They are bedded down each morning
With great big bales of straw,
They have silage made last summer
And rolled barley from the store.

But soon the grass is growing,
The birds sing of the spring
The sun dries up the ditches
And the farmer cuts the string.

the barn gates now fly open
and the cattle start to moo,
excitement now is mounting
you can tell that by the poo.

The first one leaps out forwards
And the others push and shove,
They can smell the new grass growing
This is the day I really love.

To see the whole herd trotting
Along the rutted track,
The young ones and the old ones
There is no going back.

As they go out through the gateway
Udders swinging to and fro',
They gallop round the hedgerows
Kicking high and low.

The joy you see at turn out
Those old cows having fun,
It's really something special
When all is said and done.

You marvel at old Gladys
She really makes you laugh,
Trotting like a young one
Prancing like a calf.

And look at dear old Mabel
rooting up the ground
grunting as she does it,
take in that happy sound.

and Bella who's the oldest
is holding her head high
munching on the daisies
then watch that udder fly!

Will this be us post lockdown
When we are all let out?
Ethel in her curlers
Dancing all about.

Bernard in his braces
Skipping down the street
Hugging friends and neighbours
Oh, won't life be so sweet.

Hang on everybody
One day turn out will come,
And we can walk together
And have fun in the sun.

Don't Block the Gate!

There are somethings you should never do out in the country and one of them is to block a gateway!

I watched them from a distance,
I'd seen it once before
I climbed the stile gently
From the field on to the moor.

A car was in a gateway
It was rocking to and fro,
Just as old Jacob Edwards
Went down the lane to mow.

Old Jacob was a farmer
And this was on his land,
He knew each tree and hedgerow
Truer than his hand.

Everyone knew Jacob
The last of a long line
And if you didn't cross him,
Well life would be just fine.

His hands were gnarled and calloused
His eyes were piercing blue,
Each wrinkle told a story
Of all that he'd lived through.

He'd done his years of courting
But let me set you straight,
He was kind and giving
If you didn't block his gate.

He was on his Massey Fergy
The one he loved to drive
He'd bought it in the sixty's
his precious 135.

The birds, they all were singing
The sun was rising high,
The perfect day for mowing
The forecast set to dry.

Jacob, he was happy
He was whistling through his teeth,
And I watched the fun unfolding
From my viewpoint on the heath.

He chugged around the corner
And then he saw the car,
He pushed back on the throttle
Before he went too far.

The couple hadn't heard him
They were bouncing up and down,
They didn't see old Jacob
Pull down his hat and frown.

He jolted on the gear stick
And changed down into low,
And the vintage finger mower
Swung wildly to and fro'.

They had blocked his gateway
So, he drove up on the bank,
And right across the valley
You could hear the crunch and clank.

The car was shaking wildly
The girl let out a cry,
The man was so ecstatic
Then he finished with a sigh.

Jacob now was mowing
He didn't even swear,
There's no excuse for blocking gateways
And he didn't have a care.

The man then drove off slowly
With a rattle and a clang,
And left behind a bumper
What a price for one short bang!

THE LADYBIRD WITH NO SPOTS

Another one for the kids. This one has an important message.

All the little ladybirds had polished up their shells
They'd counted up their spots and shone those up as well.
They looked so very happy, they couldn't get much cleaner
And everyone one was smiling apart from little Tina.

Now Tina was a ladybird who didn't have a spot
Her shell was red and gorgeous, but she didn't have a dot.
Some of the other ladybirds laughed and called her names
And Tina felt rejected, it really was a shame.

She hid behind the shadows of all the plants and leaves
She didn't like to show off and skulked amongst the trees.
She felt so sad and worried that she'd never be accepted,
She thought that she was destined to always be rejected.

And then a little beetle as plain as plain can be
Spoke to Tina quietly and said, "just look at me".
"You may be very worried because you haven't got your spots
But I'm not even shiny and I couldn't give a jot.

It really doesn't matter about the colour of your coat
And I know the other ladybirds call you names and gloat
But the thing that really matters is what is in your heart
And I know you're really clever, and you're also very smart.

You are a special ladybird, no one looks the same as you
With your coat so red and perfect it shines as good as new
Be proud that you are different, I'm sure you will agree
Then you can say out loud that there's no one else like me"!

BRING ON THE FARMERS!

This was written just before the vaccination programme started. I reckon they could have done it, don't you?

Everyone is worried,
When will we get our jab?
we're all stuck in lockdown
life has become so drab.

We should hand it to the farmers
It would only take a week,
They've had lots of practice
Injecting all those sheep.

I reckon they could do it
They've got some decent kit,
If they line up all their hurdles
They'll do it in one hit.

The ones who keep the cattle
Well, they could use a crush,
The dogs would sort the queue out
There is no need to rush.

They may even change the needle
Every hour or so,
And they will keep on going
Through wind and rain or snow.

And whilst we are together
They could even check our teeth
And fire up the shearing handsets
And give us a trim beneath!

A COUNTRYMAN

Please remember this when you are caring for elderly relatives, especially those who have spent a lifetime working outdoors.

Imagine a life spent mainly outdoors,
Where the fields are your carpets
The hedges your walls.
With the sun on your face
And the sting of the rain
Tending your flock, or planting the grain

Imagine a time when you looked to the sky
Sometimes too wet and sometimes too dry.
But the seasons roll on
and you manage the land,
if it's not in your blood
you may not understand.

Imagine a man who knows every tree
And the roll of each hill from the gate to the sea,
And the days turn to weeks
And the months into years
Of a lifetime of joy
And occasional tears.

Imagine that man as he now grows old
And he struggles to walk back out in the fold.
Then he starts to forget
All his family and friends
and he worries about
where all this will end.

Imagine that man now stuck in the house
Inside those four walls, just him and his spouse.
And she struggles to cope
As he's slipping away
And their brightly lit world
Has all turned to grey.

But deep in his soul is the murmur of trees,
The feel of the sun and the soft summers breeze.
It's all still inside
He just needs us to see,
That he wants to get out
Where he can be free.

Please don't lock him away, it will do him more harm.
Give him a chance to get back on a farm.
Remember the man
It is no disgrace,
To get mud on his boots
and a smile on his face.

ALSO BY THE AUTHOR

Tiny Caring Gestures
Gentle Sweet Reminders
Ssh... It Happens! Rural Rhymes from Ryme Intrinseca
Ssh... It Happened Again! More Rural Rhymes
Recent Rhyming Rambles
Quad Bike Style